P9-DHI-218

THE
# NEW PARENTS'
# BOOK OF FIRSTS:
## THE SEEMINGLY INSIGNIFICANT
## BUT TRULY ASTOUNDING
## ACCOMPLISHMENTS
## OF MOM AND DAD

By Lane Walker Foard

CHRONICLE BOOKS
SAN FRANCISCO

FOR NICOLE, COOPER, AND RILEY
who (along with food, clothing, and shelter) are my basic needs.

Text © 2004 Lane Walker Foard
Illustrations © 2004 Debbie Hanley

All rights reserved. No part of this book may be reproduced in any
form without written permission from the publisher.

ISBN 0-8118-4357-2

Design by Alethea Morrison
Manufactured in China

Distributed in Canada by
Raincoast Books
9050 Shaughnessy Street
Vancouver, B.C. V6P 6E5

Chronicle Books LLC
85 Second Street
San Francisco, CA 94105
www.chroniclebooks.com

10 9 8 7 6 5 4 3 2

Visit www.squibnocketville.com for more information on the author
and Squibnocket Cards.

SQUIBNOCKET
unintentionally consequential since 1999

## WELL, WELL, WELL.

It appears you and your loved one have pulled the blinds, pushed the twin beds together, and commingled your genetic material. And now, sweet mother of all that's good and pure, you got yourselves a baby. Congratulations. To say everything's going to be new and different from this moment on is to engage in a big honking understatement.

Welcome to parenthood. Every day your baby will do something new, and you'll find plenty of albums to record all of it. However, as a new parent, you'll do something new every day, too—from engaging in saliva-based hygiene to exaggerating your child's accomplishments. Seriously. This book is for you, new parents, and all your illustrious firsts, both big and small.

## THE FIRST TIME WE CAME HOME FROM THE HOSPITAL

and thought, "Sweet mother of Abraham Lincoln, we got ourselves
a real live baby here."

[DATE:                    ]

_____

_____

_____


## THE FIRST TIME DAD CHANGED A DIAPER

without announcing it and looking for praise from Mom.

[DATE:                    ]

_____

_____

_____

## THE FIRST TIME MOM AND DAD LOOKED AT THE PERFECT,

smiling, rested couple pictured on the box that the high chair
came in and thought, "We're nowhere near as happy as they are."

[DATE:                    ]

## THE FIRST TIME MOM AND DAD ENGAGED IN THE

back-and-forth opera of semi-conscious but fully cognizant
snorts and moans to suggest that each was still asleep when the baby
started crying at four in the morning.

[DATE:                    ]

## THE FIRST TIME MOM AND DAD REALIZED

that the four best words in the history of the English language are
"sleeping through the night."

[DATE: ]

_____

_____

_____


## THE FIRST TIME WE REALIZED THAT NO MATTER WHAT

(even if the Prize Patrol van pulls up in our driveway), we should
never, ever, ever wake up a sleeping baby.

[DATE: ]

_____

_____

_____

## THE FIRST TIME MOM OR DAD HAD A CONVERSATION WITH

the baby using the "Inquisition of Who's," as in, "Who's the cutest baby?"
or "Who's Mama's favorite little baby?" or "Who's gotta go poopy?"

[DATE:                    ]  _____

_____

_____

_____


## THE FIRST TIME DAD MOMENTARILY REMOVED HIMSELF

from his body to witness himself doing the extraordinarily embarrassing,
entirely nonmasculine, fingers-spread-out clap in front of the baby.

[DATE:                    ]  _____

_____

_____

_____

## THE FIRST TIME MOM REMINDED DAD

that his "sympathetic weight gain" during her pregnancy must now, by
standard rules of logic, be followed by his "sympathetic weight loss."

[DATE:                    ]

_____

_____

_____


## THE FIRST TIME DAD REALIZED THAT IN THE GREAT

bottle-feeding vs. breast-feeding debate, the fact that only
Mom is able to breast-feed is extremely important (albeit profoundly
selfish) to his own quantity of sleep.

[DATE:                    ]

_____

_____

_____

MEMORIAL PHOTO OF SINGLE FRIENDS WE
NO LONGER DO ANYTHING WITH.

## THE FIRST TIME MOM OR DAD READ *GOOD NIGHT MOON*
and thought, "Jeez, I could've written this."

[DATE:            ]

## THE FIRST TIME DAD REALIZED THAT HE'S NEVER
experienced any more panicked and stressful minutes than the ones spent
looking for the crying baby's lost pacifier.

[DATE:            ]

## THE FIRST TIME MOM REALIZED, MUCH TO HER IMMEASURABLE

chagrin, that she's starting to act and sound just like her mother.

[DATE:                    ]

___

## THE FIRST TIME DAD STRATEGICALLY FIGURED OUT

the baby's pooping schedule so that his turn always seems to fall on a
pee diaper and Mom's turn falls on a poop one.

[DATE:                    ]

## THE FIRST TIME AN ANNOYING TELEMARKETER CALLED

while our baby was crying and one of us held the phone out and said,
"You hear that? You did that, mister. I hope you're happy with yourself."

[DATE:              ]

_____

_____

_____

## THE FIRST TIME WE HURRIEDLY PAID FOR

and then abandoned an uneaten meal in a restaurant because our baby
wouldn't stop crying.

[DATE:              ]

_____

_____

_____

PHOTO OR SKETCH OF FAVORITE ARTICLE
OF CLOTHING NOW RUINED.

## THE FIRST TIME ONE OF US UNDERSHOT

our baby's true age by several months when someone asked, so as to make him appear more advanced than he should be.

[DATE: ]

_____

_____

_____

## THE FIRST TIME MOM CAUGHT DAD SHAMELESSLY USING

the baby to talk to a completely hot woman who, under standard circumstances, wouldn't look at him even if his hair were on fire.

[DATE: ]

_____

_____

_____

## THE FIRST TIME MOM OR DAD STEPPED ON

a pain-inducing plastic baby toy in the dark and quickly replaced a
swear word with a G-rated, faux swear word.

[DATE:                    ]

_____

_____

_____

## THE FIRST TIME WE HAD A SERIOUS

and entirely unapologetic dinner-table conversation about poop.

[DATE:                    ]

_____

_____

_____

## THE FIRST TIME WE WENT TO RIDICULOUS LENGTHS

to get our crying baby to fall asleep (i.e., drove around the neighbor-
hood at four in the morning while wearing robes).

[DATE:                ]

## THE FIRST TIME WE WAVED AT OTHER NEIGHBORHOOD

parents doing the same thing.

[DATE:                ]

## THE FIRST TIME DAD REALIZED THAT IN ABOUT FOUR YEARS

his baby will want to have a superhero birthday party, and Dad
will, as Dads must, dress up (in front of other parents, mind you) in the
sleek, leave-nothing-to-the-imagination, superhero leotard costume
that will look like someone just shrink-wrapped a stack of snow tires.

[DATE: ]

_____

_____

_____

## THE FIRST TIME MOM UNCONSCIOUSLY DRESSED

the baby exactly like herself.

[DATE: ]

_____

_____

_____

## THE FIRST TIME WE REALIZED THE FBI

may want to put our baby's cry on loudspeakers for use in standoffs
with militia compounds.

[DATE:                    ]

## THE FIRST TIME DAD SECRETLY TURNED ON THE BABY MONITOR

and, in the mimicked voice of the baby, said something to the
effect of, "Mommy, could you be a dear and bring me some more milk."

[DATE:                    ]

## THE FIRST TIME MOM WATCHED A SPEEDING CAR

on our street and shouted, "Slow down! Kids live around here!" even though she, just weeks ago, was driving exactly the same way.

[DATE:                       ]

_____

_____

_____

## THE FIRST TIME DAD WATCHED THE BABY

coat the remote control with saliva or throw up on his good jacket but was too paralyzed with love to be able to do anything about it.

[DATE:                       ]

_____

_____

_____

## THE FIRST TIME WE REALIZED THAT FOR AT LEAST THE NEXT
eighteen years, we will never be anywhere in twenty minutes.

[DATE: ]

_____

_____

_____

_____


## THE FIRST TIME WE REALIZED THAT WE WILL NEVER AGAIN
in our lifetime need an alarm clock or the snooze button.

[DATE: ]

_____

_____

_____

_____

HANDWRITING SAMPLE TAKEN DURING EARLY MORNING HOURS
AFTER ONE WEEK AS SLEEP-DEPRIVED PARENT.

HANDWRITING SAMPLE TAKEN DURING EARLY MORNING HOURS
AFTER ONE MONTH AS SLEEP-DEPRIVED PARENT.

## THE FIRST TIME WE HAD THAT PROUD

yet slightly shameful internal feeling that our baby is more attractive
than someone else's baby.

[DATE:                    ] _____

_____

_____

_____


## THE FIRST TIME MOM OR DAD TOLD A COMPETITIVE LIE

to another parent regarding our child's accomplishments, as in, "Yeah,
well, my baby was walking when he was only seven months old."

[DATE:                    ] _____

_____

_____

_____

RECEIPT FROM LAST PRE-BABY
GROCERY SHOPPING TRIP.

RECEIPT FROM FIRST POST-BABY
GROCERY SHOPPING TRIP.

## THE FIRST TIME MOM'S BLOUSE LEFT THE HOUSE CLEAN

and returned home clean after an entire day out with the baby.

[DATE:                    ]

_____

_____

_____

_____

## THE FIRST TIME MOM HAD A POST-BIRTH ADULT BEVERAGE

and immediately got so loopy Dad had to shuffle her home
before she climbed on a table and started singing her show-tune version
of "The Wheels on the Bus Go Round and Round."

[DATE:                    ]

_____

_____

_____

_____

## THE FIRST TIME MOM OR DAD ENGAGED IN SALIVA-BASED
hygiene on the baby (face cleaning or hair grooming).

[DATE:                  ]

_____

_____

_____

## THE FIRST TIME WE CAME HOME FROM A DAY OUT
with the baby and realized, as other parents have since time
immemorial, that a sock had somehow disappeared.

[DATE:                  ]

_____

_____

_____

_____

## THE FIRST TIME WE FINALLY ASSEMBLED THE PORT-A-CRIB
in less than forty minutes.

[DATE: ]

## THE FIRST TIME MOM OR DAD WAS FORCED TO SIZE UP
a complete stranger's baby, determine he was about the same size as
ours, and ask to borrow a diaper.

[DATE: ]

PHOTO OF MOM OR DAD MAKING A DOWNRIGHT
UNNECESSARILY RIDICULOUS GOO-GOO FACE FOR THE BABY.
(NOTE REMARKABLE FACIAL SIMILARITIES TO MOMENT
OF BABY'S CONCEPTION.)

## THE FIRST TIME WE LEFT THE BABY WITH A SITTER,

drove around the block, and returned home after five minutes because,
"The baby's just not ready for that yet."

[DATE: ]

_____

_____

_____

_____

## THE FIRST TIME DAD REALIZED THAT HIS MASCULINITY

quotient is slowly being chipped away with the necessary employment of
words such as "onesie," "binky," "blankie," and "sippy cup."

[DATE: ]

_____

_____

_____

_____

## THE FIRST TIME WE LOADED UP OUR CAR WITH SO MUCH

baby gear that we looked like that westward-bound truck in *The Grapes of Wrath*, only to be taking a day trip to the grandparents' house.

[DATE: ]

_____

_____

_____

_____


## THE FIRST TIME MOM SUCCESSFULLY PERFORMED

the all-important "reach back" maneuver to find and replace the baby's pacifier while driving, all without taking her eyes off the road.

[DATE: ]

_____

_____

_____

_____

## THE FIRST TIME MOM OR DAD SLIPPED A NOTCH
down the Parenting Perfection Ladder from hyper-sterilizing a dropped
pacifier to just rinsing it off in the sink.

[DATE:                    ]

## THE FIRST TIME MOM OR DAD SLIPPED EVEN FURTHER
down the Ladder from rinsing off a dropped pacifier to just blowing on it.

[DATE:                    ]

## THE FIRST TIME DAD NOTICED THAT THE ARM

on the car-seat-carrying side of his body has become so overdeveloped
that when he's not carrying it, he actually pulls slightly in that direction.

[DATE: _____ ]

_____

_____

_____

_____

## THE FIRST TIME MOM YELLED THE BABY'S NAME

out the back door at dinnertime, "Just to test out what it sounds like."

[DATE: _____ ]

_____

_____

_____

_____

## THE FIRST TIME MOM OR DAD TOUCHED SOMETHING

that looked completely dry but in actuality was soaking wet with drool.

[DATE:                ]

## THE FIRST TIME MOM HAD THAT SEEMINGLY UNIQUE

(but apparently amazingly universal) thought about starting
her own line of baby clothes, only to have the epiphany thwarted
by a constant state of extreme sleep deprivation.

[DATE:                ]

MISSING-PERSONS PHOTO OF HAPPY, FIT, RESTED COUPLE
THAT HASN'T BEEN SEEN SINCE THE BABY'S BIRTH.

## THE FIRST TIME DAD WAS OUT WITH FRIENDS

and caught himself making siren sounds out loud when a fire truck
drove by—even though the baby was back at home.

[DATE:                    ]

_____

_____

_____

_____


## THE FIRST TIME WE PUBLICLY REFERRED TO OURSELVES

as "Mom and Dad" without feeling like we were playing make-believe.

[DATE:                    ]

_____

_____

_____

_____

## THE FIRST TIME MOM OR DAD REALIZED

that there is nothing louder and nothing that causes more personal
anxiety than a crying infant on a full airplane flight.

[DATE:                    ]

_____

_____

_____

_____


## THE FIRST TIME WE REALIZED THAT WE KNOW EVERY BIT

of dialogue to baby's favorite video.

[DATE:                    ]

_____

_____

_____

_____

## THE FIRST TIME MOM LOOKED AT THE LIVING ROOM'S

complete disarray and realized her threshold for cleanliness and order
had officially been recalibrated.

[DATE:                    ]
_____

_____

_____

_____


## THE FIRST TIME WE REALIZED THERE'S LITTLE TO NO POINT

of having decent furniture for at least the next three years.

[DATE:                    ]
_____

_____

_____

_____

FIRST SMALL ITEM TO SAFELY PASS THROUGH THE BABY'S
DIGESTIVE TRACT. (NOW STERILIZED, OF COURSE.)

## THE FIRST TIME WE REALIZED THAT WE NOW CONSUME

meals with the blind focus, removed enjoyment, and
raw speed of New Jersey State Fair competitive hot dog eaters.

[DATE:             ]

_____

_____

_____

## THE FIRST TIME DAD REALIZED THAT WHEN HE STRAPS ON

the papoose-style baby carrier, the baby's dangling and kicking
feet are exactly level with his unsuspecting groin (thereby revealing one
of the most painful design flaws in history).

[DATE:             ]

_____

_____

_____

## THE FIRST TIME MOM OR DAD TALKED

"babbling new parent nonsense" to the uncomprehending baby
in public without embarrassment.

[DATE:                    ]

## THE FIRST TIME MOM OR DAD FOUND A PACIFIER

in a ridiculously unpredictable place (like stuffed inside a dress shoe),
six months after last seeing it.

[DATE:                    ]

# "SO, WHAT'S IT LIKE HAVING A BABY?"

Trust us. The uninitiated are going to ask (in that naive, frightened, head-tilt way) what having a baby is like. You've been where they haven't, and they want to hear the tales, see the snapshots if you will. So here are some starter sentences to help you sum up the collective experience of parenting.

✠     ✠     ✠     ✠     ✠     ✠     ✠

"Well, there's a lot of foaming at the mouth. And erratic behavior. And abnormal facial expressions. And . . . wait, did you say, What's it like having babies? I thought you said 'having rabies.' I'm sorry, I'm just so tired these days."

✠

"Imagine the happiest, most perfect moment of your life. Now add ten. Then imagine the most exhausting, trying moment of your life. And add eleven."

✠

"Well, you know how you take an Etch-a-Sketch and turn it upside down and shake it and everything gets reset? It's sort of like that. Every day. No, sorry, every hour."

✠

"It's like a fall drive along a blissful, bucolic, perfectly paved road—like on a New England college campus. Only there's an annoying speed bump every ten feet. But oddly, in between the jarring, disproportionately numerous bumps, you somehow get up just enough speed to enjoy a perfect, exhilarating moment. It's just like that."

## THE FIRST TIME WE REALIZED THAT WE HAVE BECOME

newly converted parenting fanatics and, like annoying
time-share condo salesmen, are always passionately trying to talk
others into joining the fold.

[DATE: ]

THE ASTONISHINGLY ACCURATE

# NEW PARENT
# GROWTH,
## DEVELOPMENT, AND
## OVERALL BETTERMENT
# CHART

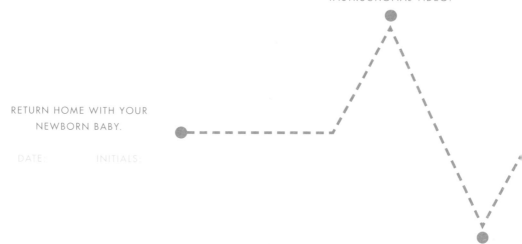

RETURN HOME WITH YOUR
NEWBORN BABY.

DATE:           INITIALS:

DATE:           INITIALS:                    CH

CHANGE FIRST DIAPER WITHOUT AID OF
INSTRUCTIONAL VIDEO.

REALIZE WITH HORROR
LULLABY YOU KNOW IS ACT
A BABY FALLING OUT O

DATE:                IN

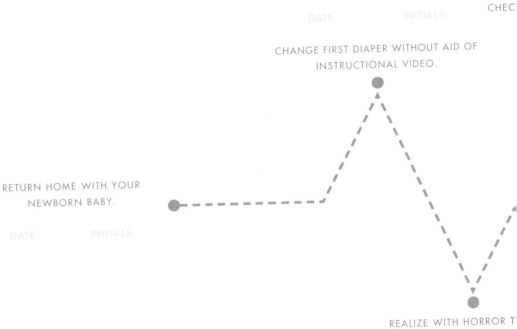

DATE:     INITIALS:

CHEC

CHANGE FIRST DIAPER WITHOUT AID OF
INSTRUCTIONAL VIDEO.

RETURN HOME WITH YOUR
NEWBORN BABY.

DATE:     INITIALS:

REALIZE WITH HORROR T
LULLABY YOU KNOW IS ACT
A BABY FALLING OUT OF

DATE:     IN

THE ASTONISHINGLY ACCURATE

# NEW PARENT
# GROWTH,
## DEVELOPMENT, AND
## OVERALL BETTERMENT
# CHART

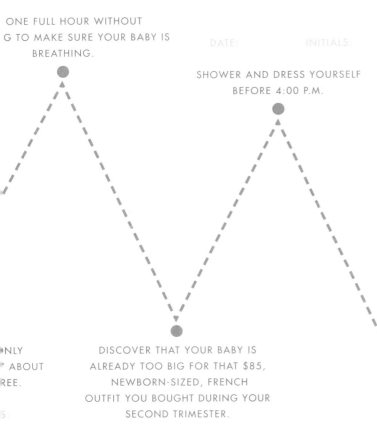

ATE:      INITIALS:

ONE FULL HOUR WITHOUT
G TO MAKE SURE YOUR BABY IS
BREATHING.

DATE:      INITIALS:

SHOWER AND DRESS YOURSELF
BEFORE 4:00 P.M.

NLY
ABOUT
REE.

S:

DISCOVER THAT YOUR BABY IS
ALREADY TOO BIG FOR THAT $85,
NEWBORN-SIZED, FRENCH
OUTFIT YOU BOUGHT DURING YOUR
SECOND TRIMESTER.

DATE:      INITIALS:

DUE TO EXTREME SLEEP DEPRIVATION,
YOU SNAP AT SPOUSE FOR CHEWING
FOOD TOO LOUDLY.

DATE:      INITIALS:

DATE: INITIALS:

SUCCESSFULLY PACK DIAPER BAG WITH
EVERYTHING YOU AND YOUR BABY
COULD POSSIBLY NEED.

DATE: INITIALS:

MOM HAS LENGTHY, INSIGHTFUL, AMAZINGLY
OPEN CONVERSATION WITH HER NEW BEST
FRIEND—ANOTHER FIRST-TIME MOM SHE MET
WHILE STROLLING WITH THE BABY.

DAD, IN PRIVACY OF HOME,
DOES THE EXTRAORDINARILY
EMBARRASSING, ENTIRELY
NONMASCULINE "YAAAAY!" CLAP
FOR THE BABY.

DATE: INITIALS:

TAKE FORTY MINUTES JUST TO GET OUT
OF THE HOUSE, TWENTY MINUTES TO
GET INTO THE CAR, AND END UP BEING
AN HOUR LATE TO YOUR DESTINATION.

DATE: INITIALS:

DAD, IN PUBLIC, DC
EMBARRASSING, E
"YAAAAY!" C

DATE: